An Invitation to Christian Yoga

Other Church Publishing Books by Nancy Roth

We Sing of God: A Hymnal for Children (1989)
Robert N. Roth and Nancy L. Roth, editors (Teacher's Guide,
Children's Hymnbook, Rudiments of Music Worksheets, and Audiotape)

Praying: A Book for Children (1991)
A Closer Walk: Meditating on Hymns for Year A (1998)
Awake My Soul: Meditating on Hymns for Year B (1999)
New Every Morning: Meditating on Hymns for Year C (2000)
Praise My Soul: Meditating on Hymns (2001) Large print edition
Tween Prayer: Friendship with God (2004)
Spiritual Exercises: Connecting Body and Spirit in Prayer (Available in March 2005)

Also by Nancy Roth
Meditations for Choir Members (Morehouse, 1999)
Organic Prayer (Cowley, 1993)
The Breath of God (Cowley, 2002)

An Invitation to Christian Yoga

revised and updated edition
of A New Christina Yoga

Nancy Roth

Drawings by Susan John Mangam, STR

SEABURY BOOKS
an imprint of
CHURCH PUBLISHING, NEW YORK

A catalog record for this book is available from the Library of Congress

ISBN: 1-59627-008-X

An Invitation to Christian Yoga is a revised and updated version of *A New Christian Yoga* published by Cowley Publications in 1989.

Scripture quotations are taken from *The New Revised Standard Version* of the Bible, © 1989, by the Division of Christian Education of the National Council of the Churches of Christ in the United Sates of America. Used by permission.

Psalm quotations are adapted from *The Book of Common Prayer*.

Church Publishing Incorporated
445 Fifth Avenue
New York, NY 10016
www.churchpublishing.org

5 4 3 2 1

IN MEMORY OF MY MOTHER,
GERTRUDE

Contents

Contents

Foreword

We are the Temple of the Living God.
Glorify God in your body.
(2 CORINTHIANS 6:16, 1 CORINTHIANS 6:20)

Our bodies are gifts and vehicles of God, integral to our being. Much attention is paid to the body in contemporary western culture. However, both in and out of the church, we tend to think of it in terms of physical fitness and beauty apart from a direct relation to God. One of the gifts of our greater knowledge of Asian religious practices has been the introduction of hatha yoga, with all its care in revealing the integrality of body and spirit.

Hatha yoga historically has been "ecumenical," crossing many religious boundaries in its use. It has not been restricted to any one theological / philosophical tradition. Many Christians today, from monks to lay people to clergy, find themselves turning to hatha yoga as a way of more fully living out an incarnational Christian faith. That faith has valued the human body as a precious divine gift worthy of Christ. For a variety of unfortunate historical reasons, however, it has never, in practice, paid systematic, positive attention to the body in spiritual formation. To the degree Christ asks us to see and share his inspirited body as itself a sign of God's loving presence with us, we could say that the body itself is a sacramental reality. "This is my body—take and eat—" incorporate into yourself my body-spirit, reveal God in your whole being.

In the wider ecumenism of the Spirit being opened for us today, we can humbly accept the wisdom gained from thousands of years of special Asian spiritual attention to the body. What makes a particular practice Christian is not its source, but its intent. If our intent in assuming a particular bodily practice is to deepen our awareness in Christ, then it is Christian. If this is not our intent in any spiritual practice, then even the reading of scripture loses its Christian authenticity. The long history of authentic spiritual Christian thought and practice has included vocabulary and methods that have originated out of many non-specifically Christian sources. A truly universal faith is free to discern the hand of God at work anywhere in God's world, and let what is seen enlarge our vision of Christ and our means of realizing that vision.

The long experience of Nancy Roth with hatha yoga practiced in a Christian context with all age groups is brought to articulate fruition in this fine book. Besides providing us with a number of simple, "do-able" exercises, she gives a context of Christian understanding and prayer that will be particularly useful for people who want to be open to God's presence through their bodily practice rather than simply take on yoga to relieve stress or other symptoms. These pages fulfill the need for a contemporary, practical guide that is well-grounded theologically and spiritually. She can help readers realize the unity of their "bodyspirit," a fine phrase of hers that keeps body and spirit properly integrated.

Roth also provides much room for the differences in our body-spirits and avoids the dangers of a rigid, dogmatic approach. Her suggestions for the execution of the exercises always leave room for alternatives. Her concrete suggestions for prayers to accompany different exercises draw them into relation to God in a gentle and helpful way, while leaving room for our own prayers or silence. She also places the exercises in an important social context that connects them with our care of the earth and its people. The accompanying illustrations by Susan John Mangam are particularly clear and sensitively drawn.

We often include simple hatha yoga practices in our spiritual formation groups at the Shalem Insititute, and it will be good at last to have a contemporary, simple, Christian-grounded text to which we can refer people. I am sure this will prove true in many other places and with many individuals who care about "glorifying God" in their bodies.

TILDEN EDWARDS

Preface

In 1989, I was persuaded by my friends and students that the time was ripe for a new book on Christian yoga, some twenty-seven years after the publication of Jean-Marie DJchanet's groundbreaking volume, Christian Yoga. Dom DJchanet introduced the practice to westerners within the Christian context of a discipline that found its origins in Hinduism. Building on that insight, my work draws on more current knowledge about the physiology of exercise and uses religious language more generally accessible to present-day Christians.

This volume is intended as a guide both for novices and proficients in the practice of yoga. People who have never included physical exercise in their spiritual practice will discover in these pages a tool for integrating body and spirit in their Christian journey. Those who already use hatha yoga for purposes of physical fitness or stress reduction will discover that they can integrate this physical discipline with their prayer. Whether we are in our youth, our middle age, or the third era of our lives, we will discover that the practices in this book will stretch both body and soul.

This book is not intended to be a comprehensive presentation of the disciplines of yoga; rather, it illustrates a way to go about doing it—or, indeed, any form of exercise. My approach to this ancient tradition was forged in the crucible of the noon hour at the parish center of Trinity Church, Wall Street, New York City, during weekly Christian yoga classes for business people. I offer some basic exercises appropriate for all levels of fitness (or lack thereof!), along with suggestions for understanding those exercises in the context of the Christian faith. For people who would like to continue with more advanced hatha yoga, these suggestions can be applied to further exercises gleaned from other yoga books or classes.

I present a theological foundation, rooted in the biblical tradition, supporting the use of yoga in Christian spiritual development. While my own journey has been greatly enriched by the wisdom of other traditions, most notably the mystical traditions of the east such as the one in which yoga was born, my particular way is the Christian way. My steps are guided by the story of God's faithfulness to the people Israel found in the Hebrew scriptures and by God's revelation in the Incarnate One, Jesus, recorded in the gospels and epistles of the early church and a living reality in the lives of Christians today.

Following a section on guidelines for the use of this book and some reflection on the importance of the breath in both yoga and prayer, I provide the reader with a series of twenty-five exercises based on hatha yoga. The illustrations, created in tandem (or "in yoga") with the text, were drawn by my friend Susan John Mangam, STR. Susan is a solitary religious and an artist who expresses through her life and art the centered, contemplative openness to God that is the intention of the yoga exercises.

The sequence of movements known as The Salute to the Sun has a section of its own. I have discovered that, in an uncanny way that helps to convince me that we all seek one God, this sequence of movements—which originated in the Hindu tradition—expresses the petitions of the Lord's Prayer and could very appropriately be called The Salute to the Son.

Instructions for progressive relaxation and suggestions for meditation follow, as well as ideas for extending the body/spirit integration into the realm of what I call Christian body prayer—a subject which will someday be the focus of another book. In addition, I offer some suggestions about using yoga practices as an embodied approach to prayer at various times and in various places. *An Invitation to Christian Yoga* is intended not merely for the half-hour or so one puts aside for intentional practice, but for all the moments of daily life that offer us opportunities to open both body and spirit to God's transforming grace.

The CD that accompanies this book will lead you through the exercises and invite you to relaxation and meditation. We hope that it helps you in the process of permitting the exercises themselves to become prayer.

Move through this book at your own pace, in your own way. Use what helps you, skip what does not. It is intended, as are most books on spiritual growth, merely as a catalyst: a catalyst for the deepening of your own relationship with the God who made us—creations both of earth and of heaven, creatures both of body and of spirit, of heart and of mind.

Acknowledgments

It is always a pleasure to work with my editor, Cynthia Shattuck, and I thank her for her enthusiastic support and intelligent guidance. I also wish to thank Cynthia Crumlish and Bernice Goulden, who first read the drafts of the manuscript and offered many valuable suggestions; my colleague the late Lee Brunner, who served as one of the models for the illustrations; my husband, Bob, who contributed more than I can enumerate to this venture, by proofreading and critiquing the manuscript and providing general good will and support; and, last but not least, my illustrator and friend, Susan John Mangam, STR, with whom it has been a privilege to create this volume.

1

What is Christian Yoga?

My own introduction to hatha yoga occurred because I was a dancer seeking a further means of becoming supple and strong. I had learned that a strenuous ballet class centered and calmed me. The physical exercise of the class was a way of processing any negative energy I might have accumulated; it is very difficult to feel depressed after having just done a series of *grands jetés* across the floor. More than that, the requirement of absolute attentiveness to what I was doing had a centering and calming effect that I could only describe as "spiritual."

When I enrolled in a local Adult School yoga class, dutifully carrying my mat to the high school gym each week, I had a similar experience: the exercise affected both my body and my spirit. Furthermore, the period of relaxation and visualization at the end of class became for me a doorway into prayer. It did not matter that we had chanted *"Om"* or that the exercises had Hindu names. My awareness of my own "incarnated-ness" drew me closer to the Incarnate One. The One I encountered, as I lay on the gym floor with my body relaxed and my mind and spirit attentive, was the God I knew in Christ Jesus. The most difficult moment of every class was hearing the instructor say, at the end of the period of relaxation, "Now become aware of the room. Move your body. Sit up." I did not want to do any of that. Instead, I was ready for a period of prayer and meditation.

I entered the General Theological Seminary with a special interest in Christian spirituality and the interface of Christianity with other spiritual traditions. I had always felt particularly at home in the Christian mystical tradition. It seemed to me that the mystics were explorers in a world every human being longs for, whether consciously or unconsciously: the "world" that is the presence of God. My own experience had taught me that the body was a powerful ally in this venture.

Yet the traditional literature of Christian spirituality yielded little guidance in terms of actual prayer practices. I found only the tradition of *hesychasm,* which taught that bodily tranquility helped to produce spiritual tranquility, or *hesychia,* as the words of the Jesus Prayer—"Lord Jesus Christ, Son of God, have mercy upon me, a sinner"—were repeated in coordination with the breath and the heartbeat. There were, of course, philosophical affirmations of the body's goodness, by St. Augustine of Hippo in the fourth century—"Is not our absorbing love of life really the soul's love for its body, a love which will haunt it until that body is returned to it risen and glorious?"—and St. Mechtild of Magdeburg in the thirteenth: "Do not disdain your body. For the soul is just as safe in its body as in the kingdom of heaven." On the other hand, the harsh spiritual practices of those centuries appear to assume the fundamental enmity, not friendship, of body and soul. Many Christian "ascetical" practices concentrated on denying or subduing the body, rather than welcoming the body as a partner and companion in prayer.

The root of "asceticism" is the Greek word *askein,* meaning "to work" or "exercise"—in other words, to *use!* It seemed to me that there was a great need for teaching about how to go about *using* the body. There needed to be a new Christian asceticism that respected the integration of body and mind and reflected both the newest research in psychology and physiology and the wisdom of other, even more ancient, spiritual traditions. That is why my discovery of the "spiritual" effects of my Adult School yoga class was a key moment both in my own growth and my usefulness as a guide to others. Well before I graduated from seminary, I began to explore the many ways to nourish the life of prayer in others, presenting prayer as a part of life, not apart *from* life, in various formats: weekly classes, retreats, workshops, and quiet days. Among these were "Christian Yoga" and "Dance Prayer" classes, to which there was an immediate and enthusiastic response. Many of my students expressed the desire for a book embodying my Christian yoga teaching, and I offer this book to them, and to all who wish this particular way—which is a way among many ways—of expressing with their bodies the prayer that is within them. It is the fruit of my own discovery—on my yoga mat on the floor of the high school gym—of the gift our brothers and sisters of another tradition have given us, as we strive to follow the way of the One who embodied God, Jesus Christ.

That way has its foundation in an understanding of the human being that can best be told by means of a story: "Then the LORD God formed an earthling *(adam)* from the dust of the ground *(adamah)* and breathed into its nostrils the breath of life; and *adam* became a living being" (Genesis 2:7). This short story, Hebrew pun and all, tells us that we are all, whether male or female, *adam:* earthlings. We are all *adam,* intrinsically bonded to the earth and its rhythms of birth and growth, life and death. We are all *adam:* in our bodies dance the same atoms as those that dance in the trees, the plants, the fish, birds, and beasts of the earth.

Yet there is within us a gift from God, a gift which we earthlings called human beings know to be precious: the gift of our life-breath. We recognize that it is more than physical breath and we know that, in some mysterious way, it holds us in life. We return to God, the source of that gift as we, literally, *"ex-pire"* at death. Beyond that physical expiration, there lies a new life filled with deeper vitality.

The earliest Hebrew creation story is theology, not science. As a description of our experience of the human condition, most of us would probably agree that it is profoundly true. *The human person is a body animated by spirit, and both are a gift of God.* In the Hebrew scriptures, human life is understood as one indivisible unity of body and spirit, which in Hebrew is expressed in the word *nefesh*. The closest equivalent we can manage in English is "bodyspirit," without a space between the words.

In a world of dividedness and fragmentation, we long for that unity. When we observe the wholehearted play of a young child, when we turn our faces skyward on a starlit summer night, when we hear music that touches the core of our being, or when we merely read of simpler times, we experience nostalgia. For what do we long?

The Hebrew creation story suggests that we long for our original created state: the integration we knew in the childhood of our race, the unity we dimly remember from our own childhood. But if we read the subsequent chapters of Genesis, we are reminded, through the drama of the Fall, that a return to childhood is impossible. We are, for better or for worse, gifted with consciousness and the capacity to choose evil as well as good. Our very freedom constantly seems to split us in two. We can never be children again, either historically as the human race or chronologically as individual members of it.

But there is good news. There is a way back—or rather, forward—and it is not through our own effort. In the Incarnation, God provides the possibility of a return to human wholeness. Although the passage that follows was originally written in Greek, I will use the Hebrew *adam,* in order to continue the creation story metaphor: "The first *adam* was from the earth, an *adam* of dust; the second *adam* is from heaven. . . . Just as we have borne the image of the *adam* of dust, we will also bear the image of the *adam* of heaven" (1 Corinthians 15:47, 49). The good news, and the way, is through the incarnation of Jesus Christ, the second *Adam.*

Incarnation is not merely a theological concept, an abstraction. The root of "incarnation" is the Latin word *carn-,* meaning "flesh." It is *God become flesh.* The way back to wholeness is Jesus Christ, God in flesh—God who, out of love for us, became a body. Jesus Christ knew the joys and frailties of *adam,* living and dying as a human on this earth. The poet Samuel Crossman writes:

My song is love unknown,
my Savior's love to me,
love to the loveless shown
that they might lovely be.
O who am I that for my sake
my Lord should take frail flesh, and die?

Jesus Christ, who carried the very life of God in his body, reminds us that we are called to do the same. Our bodies are the instruments God gives us for carrying God through our lives and through our prayer. St. Teresa of Avila's prayer expresses it well:

Christ has no body on earth now, but yours;
No hands, but yours;
No feet, but yours.
Yours are the eyes through which he is to look out
    his compassion to the world.
Yours are the feet with which he is to go about doing good.
And yours are the hands with which he is to bless us now.

We carry the life of God within our bodies. That is a gift, and a responsibility. How do we express the love of God, through our "bodyspirit," in all the actions, thoughts, and prayers that make up daily life? Just what is the relationship between our all-too-real physical selves and the spirit of God within us? Through the centuries, Christians have struggled with those questions.

St. Paul, for example, had his difficulties with young congregations who did not understand the meaning of the "bodyspirit" unity. The Christians in Corinth were so swept away by their discovery of the spirit that some of them believed that it did not matter what their bodies did, and extreme sexual libertarianism and overindulgence in food and drink, even at the Lord's Supper, were rampant. "No!" said Paul. "The body is not meant for fornication but for the Lord, and the Lord for the body" (1 Corinthians 6:13). The body is meant for the Lord, and the Lord for the body! The spirit does not free us from the body, but helps us to use our bodies in responsible living: through our worship, through our work, through all that we do before God.

Moreover, our bodies are holy places, "temples." If Paul were living now, he would call them "churches"! "Do you not know that your body is a temple of the Holy Spirit within you, which you have from God, and that you are not your own? For you were bought with a price; therefore glorify God in your body" (1 Corinthians 6:19-20).

Glorifying God in our bodies has its fruition in a life that expresses our unity of "bodyspirit." It also unites us to a greater body. As we grow in knowledge and love of the incarnate Lord, we become ever more conscious that we are not isolated human beings but part of the "body of Christ and individually members of it" (1 Corinthians 12:27). Our bodies, Paul tells us, are "members of Christ" (1 Corinthians 6:15). We are connected, in Christ, to the whole human race. And we are united with him. Breathing new unity into a divided human race is the breath of Christ, who unites in his being both the *adam* and the Creator of the creation story.

This book presents one particular way of opening ourselves to the wholeness and holiness that is the gift of God in Christ, as we seek to relearn the unity of "bodyspirit." It is the way based on hatha yoga, which was developed in the ancient Hindu tradition. Because we practice it within the Christian context, we call it "Christian yoga." The word "yoga" comes from the Sanskrit word *yug*, which means to "yoke" or "join together." For Hindus, the various disciplines of yoga help to join together body and mind, the human being and the divine, and the self and the world. Some of these practices concern devotion *(bhakti yoga)*, knowledge *(jnana yoga)*, action *(karma yoga)*, and inner concentration, called the "royal way" *(raja yoga)*. Hatha yoga is a branch of *raja yoga* and involves postures, breathing techniques, and concentration exercises, or meditation. The word *hatha* actually consists of two words: *ha*, which means "sun," and *tha*, which means "moon." The sun represents the expenditure or expression of energy; the moon, the acquiring or conservation of energy. The joining together of these principles through the exercises of hatha yoga creates a balance like that of the cosmic rhythm of the sun and moon.

Since the human body does not vary according to religion, it is not surprising that exercises which originated in Hinduism can be readily incorporated into another theological context. As we have suggested earlier, when practiced within a religion whose foundational doctrine is that of the Incarnation, the match is a natural one. In addition, since the basic approach of hatha yoga is one of recognition of and respect for the body's capabilities, it is not surprising to discover the self-same exercises and positions in many forms of physical fitness and dance training throughout the world. It is this respect for the body that makes adapting the exercises to various ages and capabilities so appropriate an enterprise.

In the English language, the words for "health" and "holiness" share the same root: the Anglo-Saxon word *hal*. Hatha yoga emphasizes the quiet body-awareness and relaxation that contribute to health; it also becomes a means of growing in the centeredness that contributes to holy living, as we unite our prayer with our bodies and our bodies with our prayer.

What *is* prayer? Prayer is more than the words we say. It is also the thoughts we bring before God. It is the attentive silence in which we wait upon God. It is life, lived with a sense of each moment as response to God. It is all the ways we respond to God by seeking to grow in relationship with God.

Have you ever intended to spend a period of time in prayer and discovered that you were distracted by a restless and uncomfortable body? The exercises and relaxation of Christian yoga may help you to become centered, so that you can attend to the words you speak, either aloud or in your heart. Yoga may help you to quiet body and mind so that you can enter into reflective prayer.

Have you ever wished that you could calm your racing thoughts so that you could just sit quietly in the presence of God? Attention to your breath can provide a mental focus so that you can become still.

Have you sought a way to remember God's presence in your daily life? Perhaps that might best be achieved by *re-membering* yourself as a member of Christ: bringing the members of your body—arms, legs, torso, and head—together, and recognizing that you are one, "bodyspirit." That is the first step to nurturing a habitual awareness that you are a living, moving temple of the Spirit.

In addition to being a preparation for prayer and for prayerful living, the disciplines of Christian yoga can themselves become prayer. Attention to the position and movement of the body can be an act of gratitude to your Creator, the one who transformed *adamah* into *adam*. "I will thank you because I am marvelously made; your works are wonderful, and I know it well" (Psalm 139:13).

Relaxing can be a physical expression of trust in the God in whom we can dependably live and move and have our being. Attentive breathing can be a kinetic meditation on the life that is the gift of the Creator within us. My prayer is that this volume may enrich *your* prayer, as you respond to the One who created you, shared human life with you, and fills you—*adam*—with the Spirit that gives you life and unites you to your companions throughout the earth, and to God.

II

Guidelines

The preceding pages have provided a theological framework for Christian yoga, so that you will be at ease spiritually in this discipline. This section provides a framework for physical ease through suggestions about space, time, tempo, clothing, and usage. Since we are "bodyspirit," these are not mere incidentals. We are affected more than we usually realize by our surroundings, and attention to the "how" and "when" of Christian yoga will facilitate our yoga practice.

Physical Setting
You will need, especially in the beginning, a space where you can be quiet and uninterrupted. Not everyone has the luxury of a separate "yoga space," but you can use an exercise mat, a small rug, or a carpet remnant to establish a sense of a special place. If you have heavy carpeting, you may wish to use a towel or piece of fabric on top of it for that purpose. Another idea is to use a small blanket folded in two, which can then turn into a warm covering during the relaxation and meditation.

It is helpful if the air is fresh and pure, as you will be focusing on breathing. If the opportunity arises, practice your yoga outdoors. You will gain a sense of connection not merely between your body and spirit, yourself and God, but between yourself and the whole creation.

Time

Give yourself "spaciousness" in time as well. Consider the time you spend in yoga as an oasis, and shed the usual pressures of getting things done. If you are concerned about finishing at a certain time, set a timer; a quartz alarm clock is best because it is quiet.

Try to practice your yoga at a regular time. You may wish to do these exercises daily. If your life is very busy, you may find it worthwhile to alternate yoga with other means of nurturing "bodyspirit" activities such as bicycling, walking, or swimming, building into those activities the same consciousness of the body's connection to the spirit's prayer that you have discovered in yoga. Such alternation of activities also has the advantage of providing you aerobic exercise—which is one of the benefits yoga does not give.

When should you do your yoga exercises? They can be done at whatever time of day suits you, but you should wait one or two hours after eating. That leaves early morning before breakfast, late morning, mid-to-late afternoon, and later in the evening. Some people have difficulty falling asleep after yoga, but others find it particularly easy!

As you try the following exercises at various times, you are likely to discover that your body's flexibility varies during the course of the day. Some exercises may be difficult first thing in the morning and easier later in the day. Don't worry about this: just make allowances for your body and do not push it to do anything beyond its capacity.

Clothing

Clothing for yoga should allow the body to move freely. Choices include leotards, warm-ups, or loose, cotton clothing. I buy my yoga clothes—loose-fitting trousers and tops—from a clothing collective that specializes in natural fabrics, but you may find sources close to home. Shoes should not be worn while doing yoga, because you will want the freedom to spread your toes and to feel the ground beneath your feet. However, unless the room is quite warm, you may want warm socks, at least for the progressive relaxation. Have a sweater handy, also, to put on at that point in your yoga practice if you need it, or use a blanket.

Attitude

More important than the physical setting, more important than the time, more important than the clothing, is the attitude you bring to your yoga practice. All these other things are, indeed, incidentals. The key to the yoga approach to exercise is that it is *inward* and *non-competitive*. For that reason, once you have learned the exercises, you should do most of them with the eyes closed, to enhance the sense of inwardness. You do not need to compete with anyone else. You do not need to compete with the illustrations in this book. Many people become discouraged about yoga before they began because of the flexible sylphs pictured in the yoga books! For that reason, we have chosen to illustrate the exercises with an ordinary human body.

Closing your eyes also helps you learn attentiveness to your body; once you have learned the exercises, your signals come from within rather than from copying someone else's movement or posture. Such attentiveness is very important, as it prevents your injuring yourself through straining. It is extremely important to stop when you feel like stopping—even in the middle of an exercise—and to adapt or omit those exercises that do not feel comfortable to you. Respect your limits.

Yoga exercises are performed at a much slower pace than most western "fitness" exercises. Take your time. There is no hurry. Think of your yoga time as an oasis: a time when you pay attention to the body God gave you, to your own deepest self, and to God. The practice of yoga should be a pleasure, not a chore. Delight in this time.

Yoga in Groups

You may wish to form a group to practice Christian yoga and meditation. Every new venture becomes easier with mutual support. The accompanying CD is ideal for use with a group.

You can also adapt the ideas in this book to hatha yoga classes at a local "Y" or school, or even at an ashram, where words from another religion might be used. If the God you recognize within is the God you know through Jesus Christ, that experience is transferable into various settings, even into those settings where God is called by other names or by no name at all.

Yoga for All Ages and Abilities

Because it is so adaptable, yoga can be done by every member of a family. For young children, the exercises, performed at a slightly quicker tempo, can be made into a game. Young children love to "meow" during The Cat and to "poke their heads up to see what the weather is" during The Cobra. In working with young children, I have seen time and time again that participating in this kind of exercise liberates spirit as well as body.

As we grow older, it is increasingly important to maintain what physical therapists call "range of motion." Certain yoga postures may, however, need to be modified. For example, if sitting on the floor cross-legged is painful for you, it is a relief to know that you can choose an alternative position. (Despite its popularity as an icon of hatha yoga, neither the "lotus position" nor the modified "lotus" are of the essence of the practice!)

For those who, because of age or disability, have difficulty getting down onto the floor, suggestions for standing or sitting in a chair are included with most of the exercises. Sometimes it is merely a matter of getting down to the floor safely and back up again. If this is the problem, we offer the following suggestion: Stand in front of a chair and, placing both hands on the chair, lower the right knee to the floor. Now lower the left knee. Bring the right hand down onto the floor. Now bring the left hand down onto the floor so that you are on your hands and knees. Now lower your hips toward the right side, until you are sitting comfortably on the floor. To get up again, reverse the process. From the sitting position, place both hands on the floor beside you and roll onto your hands and knees. Bring the left hand up to the chair, then the right. Raise the left knee so that you are on your left foot. Then raise the right knee off the floor and stand on your right foot. Now take the hands off the chair and stand straight.

Pay special attention to those exercises that emphasize alignment. If we become truly in touch with where our body weight rests on the ground as we sit, stand, or move, we are less likely to fall as we go about our daily activities. This is true throughout our lives, but it is especially important in our later years.

Yoga practice both respects the capacity of your body at any given moment and gently challenges you to extend that capacity. If you have been a Type A personality all of your life, this is an opportunity to leave behind your perfectionism. It is to your advantage not to force yourself. The good news is that by *relaxing* into each stretch, we are sending a message to our muscles to relax and lengthen.

Yoga and Healing

Many books have been written on the mysterious interrelationship of body and spirit in the process of healing. In this process, yoga can be a powerful ally. Physiologically, it is a form of exercise that is good for the body; it is believed to stimulate various glands and inner organs, as well as limber and strengthen the muscles. For those with arthritis or similar problems, it is excellent physical therapy.

During the meditation time, if you have a physical problem or illness, you can image God's healing power entering the part of your body that is less than healthy. As you breathe, visualize the breath as a ray of life-giving light. Breathe it in and focus its healing energy, letting the light absorb the illness or pain.

For everyone, yoga is a useful form of stress-reduction. It is a direct antidote to the "flight or fight response," in which the body reacts to stress in ways that may be destructive to health. Yoga helps us learn to channel the energies of the body so that we can use them constructively, to grow in health, wholeness, and holiness.

Yoga and Verbal Prayers

Some people may find it helpful to think of particular words or phrases as they perform each exercise. Therefore we have included verses from the psalms that are suggested by each position or movement.

You may also wish to repeat mentally a prayer of your own. I will suggest a few examples here, with the understanding that these are merely guidelines to encourage you to make your own connections between the movements and what they might express in words.

Movement Mantra: The Trinity. As you perform the movements, repeat mentally, "Creator, Redeemer, Sanctifier."

Spine Collapse and Stretch. "I thank you, God, that you have made me, of dust of the earth and breath of your mouth, creature of both earth and heaven."

The Butterfly. "Alleluia! The Lord is risen! In every moment of our living and dying you are with us, our Hope and our Redeemer."

Head Rolls. "God, be in my head and in my understanding."

Shoulder Rolls. "Christ's yoke is easy and his burden is light."

Spinal Twist. "O God, you encircle me with your love. Help me to know that you are before me, beside me, behind me, surrounding me."

Side Bends. "O God, help me to be pliant, so that I can move and bend with the changes and chances of life."

I encourage you to create your own prayers to use with each exercise if it is helpful for you to do so. You may wish to use the same prayer each time, or pray spontaneously. Or you may find that words are not necessary at all, even those words that are prayed silently. For many people, the positions and movements themselves become a prayer needing no words at all.

How to Use This Book and CD

We have provided three ways of learning the following exercises: the written word, the spoken word, and the visual image. Let all three guide you.

As we have said earlier, let the movement come "from the inside." The movements in these exercises originate from the natural rhythm of inhalation and exhalation. The breath within you is the source of the momentum.

The movements and postures are natural ones, not unnatural ones: they are exercises well within the scope of an ordinary, untrained body. Begin with only the first few exercises, adding others when you feel ready, but always keeping the exercises in sequence. The number of repetitions we have indicated only as a guideline. Adapt them to your own needs. Some exercises you may wish to do only once; some, several more times than we have suggested. Move slowly, and do not force anything. Keep the abdomen strong and firm, so that it will always support the lower spine, and remember to pay close attention to instructions about posture and alignment, for attention to correct placement prevents injury. Build up your abilities through the individual exercises, until you finally reach The Salute to the Sun, which comes at the end of the exercise routine. If the Salute is difficult for you, skip it.

Use this book in freedom. Adapt it to your needs and your temperament and your own unique "bodyspirit." It is merely a guidebook. Like any guidebook, it can only point you toward the territory you are to discover; it is not itself the territory. The territory is your own "bodyspirit," through which you will, I hope, glimpse a further horizon: the infinite God, the Holy Trinity.

III

Breathing

Let everything that has breath praise you.
(PSALM 150:6)

The breath, as we have seen in our introduction, is both a physical and a "spiritual" reality, in itself a yoke or *yug* between the seen and the unseen aspects of our humanity. We tend to take our breath for granted, but inhalation and exhalation keep us in life. They also symbolize the pattern of the Christian life of giving and receiving, emptying and filling, death and resurrection. Attention to breath should be integrated into all yoga practice. We should be conscious of the breathing patterns of each exercise until those patterns become second nature, for every movement has its source in the movement of the breath. Relaxation is a matter of "breathing out" our tension. Meditation begins with attention to our breathing, which becomes ever more gentle and more quiet as we relax into God's presence.

As adults, we tend to use only a small amount of our lungs' capacity. When I ask a group of adults to "take a deep breath," inevitably I see a roomful of shoulders rising, because most people think that breathing deeply means pulling in their abdomens and raising their chests. Proper breathing is just the opposite. People who study acting or singing soon learn that they need to relearn proper breathing. As students of the "bodyspirit" tool that is Christian yoga, we also need to relearn proper breathing. I say "relearn" because once we each breathed fully and completely—as babies. Our best teachers are infants. Look at a baby breathing, lying on its back; the whole torso rises and falls with each breath.

To practice breathing, begin by lying on the ground with your knees bent and the feet flat on the floor, as shown in the drawing at the beginning of this chapter. Relax, and place the hands lightly on the abdomen just below the navel. Breathe through the nostrils and imagine that the breath *originates* in the abdomen, making it necessary for the abdomen to expand gently as you inhale. You may wish to picture a round balloon expanding inside the abdomen, generating energy for the entire body. Or a fountain, not of water but of air, originating at the base of the abdomen and steadily sending its streams all the way to the tip of each limb and to the top of the head. Let the abdominal muscles relax as you let that area fill with the oxygen of life. (What is actually happening is that raising the abdomen makes it possible for the diaphragm to expand completely, enabling the lungs—which, of course, are *not* in the abdomen—to fill with air.) In inhaling, do not *try* too hard; exhalation is where you should put your effort.

When exhaling, contract the abdominal muscles up and back toward the spine as if you were pressing the air out of the abdomen. This is the part of the breath where you may at the beginning need to exert some effort. An actor friend of mine who teaches speech production tells me that incomplete exhalations may be due to our human reluctance to trust. He has trouble getting his students to exhale completely: "They keep a little air in there, just in case!" Contracting the abdomen contributes to a strong muscular "core" that helps protect your spine, not only during yoga practice, but throughout your daily activities.

When you have discovered how to breathe abdominally, practice breathing slowly and rhythmically, counting to four slowly on the inhalation and to four again on the exhalation.

When you are comfortable with that exercise, move the hands to the area on either side of the rib cage. Now, as you inhale, expand the abdomen and *then* let the rib cage expand, like a bellows. Try to expand the *back* of your rib cage, as well as the sides and front. You will feel your hands moving. As you exhale, first contract the abdominal muscles and then let the rib cage fall. If you have pictured a round balloon expanding inside the abdomen when you practiced abdominal breathing, now picture an oblong balloon, expanding and contracting as you breathe.

Finally, bring the upper chest into the movement of the breath. Let the abdomen expand first, then the rib cage, and finally the upper chest. In exhaling, let the abdomen contract, the rib cage fall, and the upper chest fall. Picture your whole torso as a giant bellows, filling and emptying.

Practice this deep breathing while counting, keeping the exhalation and inhalation the identical number of counts, pausing a moment before you change from one to another. For example, inhale "1, 2, 3, 4"—pause—exhale "1, 2, 3, 4"—pause, and so forth. Take some time either at the beginning of each yoga practice or prior to the relaxation period to take at least ten of these full breaths.

As you perform the exercises that follow, visualize the movement coming from their source, your breath. As you relax and begin to meditate following the exercises, you will notice the breath becoming slower and more shallow, as your body enters a deep state of rest. Relax and let the rhythm of your breath become the rhythm of prayer, the prayer which is attention to the One who is the source of the breath of life.

IV

Exercises

1. Movement Mantra: The Trinity

O tarry and await God's pleasure;
be strong, and God shall comfort your heart.
(PSALM 27:18)

A spoken *mantra* is a repeated word or phrase used as a prayer. I suggest that you begin and end your yoga sessions with at least three repetitions of this "movement mantra."

Sit in an easy cross-legged position, with the spine lifted toward the sky. Imagine that a string attached to the crown of the head (where a little boy might have a cowlick) is being pulled up by an invisible hand. This exercise can also be done in a standing position, seated on a chair, or kneeling on the floor.

Inhale and raise both arms forward and upward, as you look up, stretching and reaching. (This position is not unlike that of a toddler who wishes to be picked up into a parent's arms, and is appropriate for a movement expressing relationship with God, our Creator.)

Then exhale and lower the arms out to the sides at shoulder level, with the hands palms up, to form a cross. Hold them there and turn your attention toward Jesus, our Redeemer.

The third person of the Trinity, the Holy Spirit or Sanctifier, we experience both within us and among us. Inhale, and bring your hands inward toward the heart-center; then exhale and reach forward, with the palms up in a receptive position.

Do the exercise two more times.

2. Spine: Collapse and Stretch

Unless our God builds the house,
their labor is in vain who build it.
(PSALM 127:1)

This exercise can be done seated on the floor in a cross-legged position, seated on the floor with the soles of the feet together, or seated in a chair with the feet flat on the floor.

Inhale. Think of the top vertebra being pulled up to the sky by a string going right through the top of the head. Feel as if the spine is continuing to grow. (If you do this correctly, the head will be properly balanced and there will be no tension in the neck.) Let the shoulders feel heavy and relaxed. Feel the breath filling up the body as if it were traveling up the torso from the core of the abdomen.

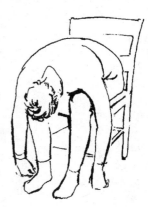

Exhale, and allow the head to fall forward, releasing the neck muscles which hold the head as you release the breath. As the head falls, the spine relaxes forward toward the floor.

Inhale. Then contract the muscles of the abdomen as you exhale and straighten the spine, vertebra by vertebra.

Repeat several times, each time feeling the head getting heavier and heavier as it falls forward, and the spine taller as it stretches toward the sky.

3. The Butterfly

O God, how manifold are your works!
in wisdom you have made them all;
the earth is full of your creatures.
(PSALM 104:25)

Seated on the floor, place the soles of the feet together. Place the hands on the ankles. Keeping the spine straight, inhale, then press the forearms lightly on the lower legs as you exhale. Release as you inhale. Press, then release, several times.

Many yoga exercises are named after animals. This one is called The Butterfly. The butterfly, whose life-cycle moves from caterpillar through cocoon through winged creature, is sometimes used as a symbol of the Resurrection. It stands for the hope of which Jesus Christ assures us even when we feel most earth-bound or imprisoned by darkness.

Alternative exercise: Seated on a chair, breathe in deeply, then exhale and raise your right knee toward your body, supporting the weight of your leg with your left hand on the ankle and your right hand under the knee. Keep the spine and straight as possible. Let the weight of the leg cause the right knee to fall gently to the right, then bring it back to the original position and lower the leg. Now do the exercise with the left leg.

Repeat on both sides.

4. Head Rolls

You have anointed my head with oil,
and my cup is running over.
(PSALM 23:5)

For this exercise, you can sit cross-legged on the floor, sit in a chair with the feet flat on the floor, or stand. Inhale. Let the head fall forward as you exhale. Relax the neck, so that the chin falls down toward the chest. Then, in a very relaxed way, roll the head slowly toward the right as you inhale so that the right ear is toward the right shoulder.

Exhale and let the head fall forward again. Inhale and roll it toward the left so that the left ear is toward the left shoulder.

Repeat at least three times.

An alternative version, which protects the cervical vertebrae in the neck, is to omit the rolling motion. Let the head drop forward and then lift it again before dropping it, first toward the right shoulder and then toward the left. Whenever the head is upright, think of it reaching toward the ceiling, and inhale. Exhale as you let it drop forward or to each side.

5. Shoulder Rolls

God satisfies you with good things,
and your youth is renewed like an eagle's.
(PSALM 103:5)

Seated cross-legged on the floor, in a chair, or standing, feel your spine reaching up toward the sky. Let the shoulders feel very heavy.

Now bring the shoulders up toward the ears. Pull them back as far as you can, and let them fall. Bring them forward, and up again, so that you have made a full circle. Repeat the circle twice.

Then reverse the circle, bringing the shoulders up toward the ears, then forward, down, and back. Repeat twice.

Throughout the exercise, inhale as you bring the shoulders upward and exhale as you release them downward.

6. Spinal Twist

I have set you always before me;
because you are at my right hand I shall not fall.
(PSALM 16:8)

Sit in an easy cross-legged position on the floor with the right leg on top of the left, or in a chair with the feet flat on the floor. Feel the bottom of the hip-bones (the "sit-bones") in contact with the floor or chair and the spine growing up toward the sky.

Inhale. Then, still feeling pulled up and tall, exhale and turn your shoulders to the right, letting the whole body follow the movement, and look behind you. Let the left arm and shoulder follow the twist. If you are seated on the floor, place the left hand on the right knee and the right hand behind you at the waist. If you are seated on a chair, place the left hand on the right side of the waist and reach around the back of the chair with the right hand.

Returning to the initial position facing forward, spend a moment being aware of the spine reaching upward, letting the shoulders hang heavy and loose and the hands rest palms down on the knees. Then, if you have been sitting cross-legged, cross the legs the other way, placing the left leg on top of the right, and turn to the left, performing the exercise to the other side. Repeat once more to each side.

This is an exercise which is performed with the eyes open. It can even become a "seeing meditation," if you really take time to gaze in each direction as you turn slowly and let your eyes rest upon each object in turn.

33

7. Rear Arm Lifts

You have put gladness in my heart,
more than when grain and wine and oil increase.
(PSALM 4:7)

This exercise can be done either seated on the floor in a cross-legged position, seated on a bench or stool (not a chair), or standing. It opens and
stretches the chest area.

If you are seated, place the hands on the knees, palms down.

Feel the spine reaching tall. Inhale and open the arms to the sides and
bring them to the back. Exhale and clasp the hands behind you. Now imagine that someone is pulling them diagonally down and out, at an angle away
from your body, and look up as you inhale.

Then imagine that they are being pulled up (like a pump handle), exhale,
and let the head drop and your body fall forward as your arms rise.

Bring the body erect again, inhaling as you lower the arms, unclasp the
hands, and return to your original position. Let the head fall forward to
relax the neck as you exhale.

8. Seated Forward Bends

I will bow down before your holy temple in awe of you.
(PSALM 5:7)

Sit on the floor with both legs stretched out directly in front of you and the spine straight, reaching and growing toward the sky. Bend the left leg and place the sole of the left foot against the right leg, somewhere between the knee and the thigh—wherever it is comfortable for you—letting the left knee drop outward. Try to feel both "sit-bones" square on the floor.

Inhale and lift both arms in front of you and up above your head, looking upward. Then exhale and reach with the chest toward the extended leg. Contract the abdominal muscles and bend at the hips, with your arms reaching toward the right foot. Breathe normally and rest in that position, letting your body relax toward the extended leg without any strain. (Paradoxically, you will find that the less you *try* to stretch, the more flexible you will eventually become.) Feel the heaviness of your head and your shoulders and imagine that there is a hinge releasing at the base of your spine so that your body can sink lower and lower toward the leg.

Inhale, contract the abdominal muscles, and return to the original position, with the arms stretching up toward the sky. Change legs, and bend toward the left leg.

Repeat the exercise again, first with the right leg stretched in front, then with the left leg in front.

(A valuable alternative exercise that can be done in a standing position is the Modified Runner's Lunge, page 74.)

9. Seated Side Bends

*You wrap yourself with light as with a cloak
and spread out the heavens like a curtain.*
(PSALM 104:2)

Seated on the floor, open the legs in a wide "V" while trying to keep the spine as straight as possible. It is more important to keep the spine straight than to open the legs wide, so adapt the "V" to your own body. Feel the bottom of the "sit-bones" squarely on the floor. Inhale and bring your arms up in front of you and up above the head, stretching toward the sky.

Exhale, and bend and reach a little forward and then toward the right, so that the right ear drops toward the right knee. Do not let your spine roll back, but keep your weight in front of the "sit-bones." The right arm touches the right leg or foot and the left arm reaches over the head toward the right. Inhale, and come back to the original position, stretching toward the sky.

Exhale, and bend a little forward and toward the left, with the left ear toward the left leg and the arms reaching toward the left. Inhale, and come back to the original position. Repeat to each side.

Then repeat the exercise, this time turning the torso as you reach down toward the leg, so that the *forehead,* rather than the ear, goes down toward the knee. Place the hands gently on the leg toward which you are stretching. Perform this variation twice to each side.

An alternative exercise is Standing Side Bends, described on page 61.

10. The Cat, #1

...like a young lion lurking in secret places.
(PSALM 17:12)

Begin on your hands and knees with your back flat. Inhale, then arch your spine upward as you exhale, thinking of pressing the small of your back as high as possible. Remember that your neck is part of the spine; as you arch upward, tuck your head between your arms. Think of bringing the forehead and the pubic bone as close together as possible.

Then reverse the curve. Inhale and press the back downward, and look upward, with the chin and the tailbone both reaching up toward the sky.

Repeat at least three more times. The movement should be gentle, feline, and enjoyable.

This is a valuable exercise for those with back problems. If you have difficulty getting down onto the floor, review the directions on page 12.

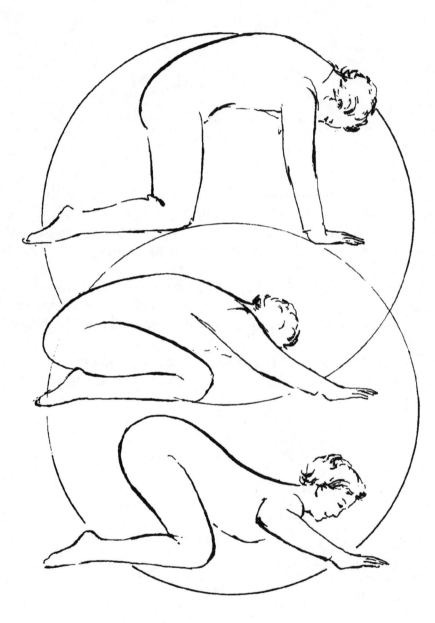

11. The Cat, # 2

The lions roar after their prey
and seek their food from God.
(PSALM 104:22)

Begin on the hands and knees, with the back flat. Inhale, then arch the spine as you exhale. Then, without moving the hands from their original position, move the body backward, bringing the buttocks down toward your feet and sitting on your heels.

Now, while you inhale, move the chest forward, keeping the elbows off the ground and moving the chest as close to the floor as possible. When your shoulders are over your hands, straighten the arms and return to the original position.

Repeat this exercise at least three more times, trying to make it as smooth as possible, like an ocean wave.

12. The Cobra

For you satisfy the thirsty
and fill the hungry with good things.
(PSALM 107:9)

Lie on your stomach on the floor, with the chin tucked under and the forehead on the floor. Place the hands on either side of the shoulders, palms down and elbows off the floor. Do *not* push hard with your hands in this exercise, but use the hands mainly for stability.

Inhale. Now use the back muscles to raise the head and upper back as you exhale. Arch the back until the navel *just* starts to come off the floor. Tilt the pelvis as if someone were pressing your tailbone downward, to prevent lower back compression. Hold for a couple of seconds, then return, tucking in the chin so that the forehead touches the floor and the back of your neck is stretched.

As you become accustomed to this exercise, you will lift the back a little more, but be sure to use the hands primarily to stabilize you, not to push upward. Keep the shoulders down and the elbows bent. Think of the *upper* back curving, rather than the waist.

In this exercise, especially, it is important not to strain for "results," but to acknowledge your own body's capability.

(An alternative exercise is the Easy Back Bend on page 71.)

13. Folded Leaf and Back Rolls

Like a child quieted upon its mother's breast,
my soul is quieted within me.
(PSALM 131:3)

After the Cobra, it is very important to bend the spine the opposite way from what you have just been doing. Choose one of the exercises below to follow the Cobra:

After you finish the Cobra, push yourself up onto your hands and knees, and then sit back on your heels. Then fold your body over, with the chest on the thighs, the buttocks on the feet, and the head bent down over the knees. Place the arms along the body down to the sides, and just rest in this posture. Notice that, when you breathe abdominally, you can feel the breathing against the thighs. This helps to relax the lower back. You can, if you wish, massage the spine with your hands as you rest.

Or: Roll over onto your back, bend your knees, and "hug" your knees to your chest. You can include the neck in the curve by bringing your forehead up to your knees. You can let the floor gently massage your back, by rolling back and forth, or side to side, in this position.

Or: Repeat the exercise on page 25 (Spine: Collapse and Stretch) seated in a chair, taking extra time to relax forward with the back rounded.

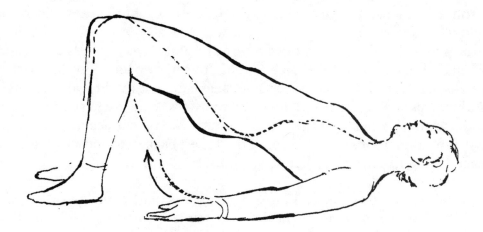

14. Pelvic Tilt

I will thank you because I am marvelously made;
your works are wonderful, and I know it well.
(PSALM 139:13)

Lie on your back with the knees bent and the feet flat on the floor. Inhale, and, as you exhale, press the small of your back into the floor by drawing the abdominal muscles in and up. Hold it there for a couple of seconds, and then release. Repeat.

Now, after you press the small of the back into the floor, continue the movement so that you raise the buttocks off the floor. Continue raising the buttocks, until you are supported by the soles of your feet. The next part of your back that touches the floor is your shoulder blades. (With practice, you may be able to extend the Pelvic Tilt into the Bridge posture, in which you roll up all the way to your shoulders.) Feel the front of the hip bones reaching upward.

Hold the position for a moment, and then roll down slowly, one vertebra at a time, beginning at the top of the spine. When you are back down, roll the head gently side to side to relax the neck.

Repeat at least once more.

You can also do the first part of this exercise seated in a straight chair. Contract the abdomen as you press your spine against the back of the chair.

15. Leg Lifts

Send out your light and your truth, that they may lead me,
and bring me to your holy hill and to your dwelling.
(PSALM 43:3)

Lying on your back, with the knees bent and feet flat on the floor, inhale and flex the toes of the right foot. Flex the whole right foot; then straighten the leg by sliding the heel out along the floor as you exhale. When the right leg is straight, tighten the abdominal muscles and raise the leg toward the sky, with the foot still flexed. The movement should be smooth and not too fast.

Inhale and bring the knee down toward the chest, keeping the foot flexed and parallel to the ceiling, as if you were trying to balance a book on the sole of the foot. Straighten the leg upward again as you exhale.

Now point the toe. Lower the leg slowly, trying to keep the small of the back on the floor. When the right leg is on the ground, inhale and slide the heel along the floor toward the body until the right leg is again bent beside the left leg.

Repeat the exercise with the left leg, and then again with each leg.

Remember that, in all leg lifts, it is the abdominal muscles that do most of the work. Contract them, as in the beginning of the pelvic tilt, and always keep the small of the back on the floor.

(Standing and seated versions of this exercise are described on page 74.)

16. Side Leg Lifts

Open for me the gates of righteousness;
I will enter them; I will offer thanks to God.
(PSALM 118:19)

Lie on the right side, keeping the body in as straight a line as possible from the top of the head to the toes. Bend the right arm, leaning the upper arm and elbow on the floor, and let the head rest on the palm of the hand. Place the left palm on the floor slightly in front of the chest in order to steady yourself. If you have trouble keeping your balance in this position, you may bend your right leg slightly behind you.

Now, keeping the left leg turned in and the left foot flexed, raise the leg moderately slowly toward the sky.

Lower the leg.

Repeat the exercise.

Change sides by curling up, hugging the knees, and rolling over to the left side. Perform the exercise twice on this side.

(An alternative exercise, Standing Side Leg Lifts, is described on page 74.)

17. Leg Bends

*As the deer longs for the water-brooks,
so longs my soul for you, O God.*
(PSALM 42:1)

Lying on your back with the legs stretched out on the floor, inhale. Then exhale and bend the right knee, bringing it up to the chest. "Hug" the knee while straightening the left leg as much as possible, then straighten the right leg out to the original position as you inhale.

Repeat with the left leg, and then again with each leg.

You may wish to vary this exercise by bringing the head up to touch the knee as it bends toward the chest, if this does not cause a strain on the neck.

Alternative exercise: Seated in a chair, breathe in deeply, then exhale and raise your right knee to your chest. Wrap your arms around your leg and squeeze your thigh to your chest and abdomen. Then lower your leg to the floor as you inhale. Repeat with the left leg.

Repeat on both sides.

18. Reaching Past the Knees

I love you, O God my strength,
You are my stronghold, my crag, and my haven.
(PSALM 18:1)

Lying on the floor with the knees bent and feet flat on the floor, inhale. Then exhale, raise the head, and look at the knees. Notice how firm the abdominal muscles become as you raise your head.

Now repeat the exercise, raising the arms about two inches off the floor and reaching forward toward the feet. As you do so, your shoulders come off the ground.

Hold the position for a few moments, then roll the spine back down, thinking of placing each vertebra in turn on the floor.

Repeat the exercise.

Then relax on the floor with knees bent, gently rolling the head from side to side to relax the neck muscles.

This is a useful exercise for strengthening the abdominal muscles. You can also strengthen them by becoming aware of them and pulling them up and in at any time of the day!

19. Standing Stretch to Sky

Lift up your hands in the holy place and bless our God;
the One who made heaven and earth bless you out of Zion.
(PSALM 134:2)

Stand with the weight equally distributed between the feet. Inhale and bring both arms straight out in front of you and then up toward the sky, stretching the whole body upward. Hold for a moment, then exhale and lower the arms in front of you, letting them hang heavy and loose at your sides. Repeat.

Stretch the arms forward again toward the sky. Now, breathing normally and keeping both arms above your head, stretch the right arm more than the left so that there is a stretch along the whole right side of the body. Then stretch the left arm, so that the left side of the body is stretched. Repeat the stretch several times, alternating your arms.

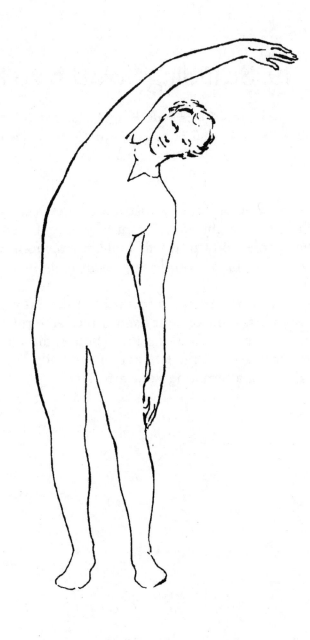

20. Standing Side Bends

You are at my side, therefore I will not fear.
(PSALM 118:6)

Stand with the feet approximately twelve inches apart. Inhale and raise the right arm out to the right side and up above the head, as if drawing a large semicircle in the air.

When your right hand is directly over your head, exhale and stretch the body toward the left, so that the left hand slides down the left side of the leg and the right hand stretches and reaches toward the left.

Inhale and straighten the body, bringing the right hand back to its original position at the side again by tracing a semicircle in the air.

Now perform the exercise to the right side, using the left arm to stretch toward the right.

Repeat on both sides.

21. Swinging Twist

And so will we never turn away from you;
give us life, so that we may call upon your name.
(PSALM 80:17)

Stand with feet solidly in contact with the ground, about eight inches apart. Feel the spine pulling toward the sky.

Now begin swinging your arms around you, first to one side and then the other, looking behind you first to one side and then to the other. Let the arms become very loose, like the arms of a rag doll. The hands will probably knock against the body.

This exercise should be performed in a very relaxed way. Continue for at least ten swings.

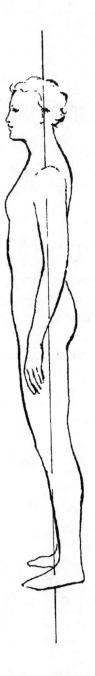

22. Alignment

Peace be within your walls and quietness within your towers.
(PSALM 122:7)

Stand with the feet directly under the hips, about six to eight inches apart. Now think of the body as a series of building blocks. The first block, which is the foundation, is the feet. Rock back and forth on the soles of the feet, feeling the contact of the feet with the floor. Think of each foot as a tripod, made up of the heel, the pad of the big toe, and the pad of the little toe. Center your weight just in front of the ankle.

The next building block is the lower part of the torso. Find the hip joints—where, if you were a wooden doll, your leg would be attached by a peg to the torso. Move the hips forward and back, until you feel the hip joints directly over the balls of the feet.

Then move the shoulder joints (where, if you were a wooden doll, your arms would be attached to the torso) over the hip joints. If the three points—the centers of the feet, the hip joints and the shoulder joints—were connected with a line, that line would be exactly perpendicular to the floor.

Now place the head correctly. Think of an imaginary string attached to the top vertebra; imagine an invisible hand pulling the string toward the sky. The string would emerge from the skull toward the back of the head, at the crown. Feel the back of the neck stretching and growing. The front of the neck is relaxed.

Now press against the floor with the front part of the feet so that the heels rise. Feel your toes spreading and clinging to the floor. Hold the position for a moment, then lower the heels slowly.

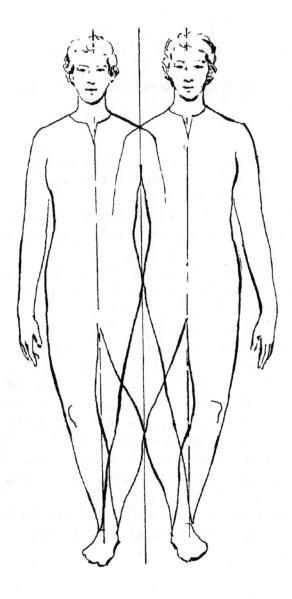

23. Weight Shifts

They are like trees planted by streams of water,
bearing fruit in due season, with leaves that do not wither.
(PSALM 1:3)

Stand in proper alignment, with the feet directly below the hips, about six to eight inches apart. Without disturbing the alignment, bend the knees slightly. Feel the weight sinking into the floor, but keep the perpendicular line between the centers of the feet, the hip joints, and the shoulder joints, and feel the counter-pull of the head pulling toward the sky. Be sure the weight is evenly divided between the two feet. You may wish to picture yourself as an accordion being pressed straight down toward the floor, with only the knees folding like a pleat.

Now shift the weight of the body to the right. The body remains straight and does not bend either backward, forward, left, or right. Raise your left foot slightly off the floor for a moment in order to check your balance.

Bring the weight back to center. Now shift it to the left, and raise the right foot slightly off the floor for a moment to check your balance.

When this becomes easy, take a *step* to the right and then center the weight over the right foot; then bring the left foot beside the right foot and center the weight between both feet.

Repeat to the left. Keep the knees pliable and relaxed, and the head on one level, without any bouncing up and down as you move. The movement is smooth, and you should have a sense of being in contact with the ground underneath your feet.

24. Standing Forward Bend

Your way, O God, is holy; who is so great a god as our God?
(PSALM 77:13)

Standing in proper alignment with feet slightly apart, inhale and bring the arms straight forward with the palms down, and up above the head, stretching toward the sky.

As you exhale, stretch the arms and the body forward, then let the head drop, the spine relax and curl down, and the arms dangle. Keep the weight on the centers of the feet, if possible, and do not "lock" or hyperextend the knees. Let the body hang for a few moments, as you inhale and exhale normally.

Then contract the abdominal muscles and roll the spine back up. Imagine your spine as beads on a string, with each vertebra falling back into place, until you are in standing position, with the head reaching to the ceiling and the arms hanging loosely at the sides.

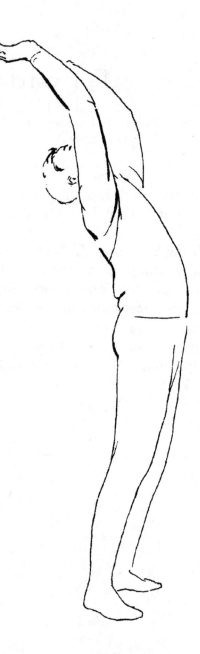

25. Easy Back Bend

To you I lift up my eyes,
to you enthroned in the heavens.
(PSALM 123:1)

Stand in good alignment, thinking especially of the hip joints and the weight of the pelvis directly over the centers of the feet, the abdomen pulled in and very flat, and the buttocks tight.

Inhale and raise the arms out in front of you (palms down) and up above your head in a big arc. When you are stretching toward the sky, continue the arc backward a short distance, imagining that the very top of your spine—the area between your shoulder blades—is curving over a small barrel. Keep the head between the upper arms. Do not "break" at the waist, but bend only at the top of the spine.

Exhale, and straighten the body, bringing the arms up above you again, in front of you and back down to your sides. Let them hang and relax, and let the head relax forward. Repeat.

When you are adept at this exercise, you can combine it with the preceding exercise by stretching backward before you perform the Forward Bend.

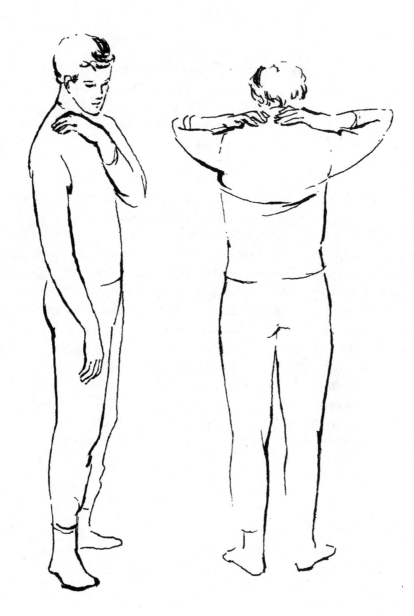

A Note About Massage

There is a river whose streams make glad the city of God,
the holy habitation of the Most High.
(PSALM 46:5)

It is important for you to pay attention to your own body's messages, and to feel free to pause at any time to incorporate gentle massage of the muscles and joints in your yoga practice. Particularly if any part of the body is stiff or sore, massage gently and slowly, thinking of the energizing and healing power that you have in your own hands.

Following certain exercises, massage is especially helpful.

Head Rolls, Shoulder Rolls, Spinal Twist: massage the back of the neck and the shoulders.

Seated Forward Bends, Seated Side Bends: massage the area around the knees, and the muscles of the calf and thigh.

Folded Leaf: massage the back muscles.

After sitting cross-legged: massage the area around the knees and the leg muscles.

Alternative Exercises

Modified Runner's Lunge

This exercise stretches the muscles in the front of the hips and back of the legs. Hold on to a chair back or lean your hands against a wall. While keeping the body upright, extend each leg behind you in turn as you bend the forward leg, in a modified "runner's lunge."

Standing Leg Lifts

Stand sideways alongside the back of a chair, holding the chair back with your left hand. Shift your weight to the left foot and inhale. Keep the abdominal muscles strong as you exhale and raise the right leg forward with the foot flexed. Then lower the leg slowly as you inhale. Repeat.

Seated Leg Lifts

Seated in a chair, grasp the chair seat with your hands and inhale. Straighten the right leg and lift it as you exhale. Then lower the leg as you inhale. Repeat with the other leg. Remember to keep your abdomen strong.

Standing Side Leg Lifts

Stand behind a chair, grasping the back with both hands. Make sure that your feet are facing forward (not turned out). Inhale, then exhale and raise your right leg to the side. Lower the leg as you inhale. Repeat the exercise twice on the other side.

V

The Salute to the Sun

From the rising of the sun to its going down
let the name of God be praised.
(PSALM 113:3)

The exercises you have just practiced can serve as a preparation for the series of movements known as The Salute to the Sun. The Salute to the Sun was traditionally performed by devout Hindus at dawn as a thanksgiving for a new day. As such, it is certainly within the realm of Christian prayer! An added dimension, however, can be added if you wish to express the petitions of the Lord's Prayer through this series of movements.

If the middle portion of the Salute to the Sun is too difficult because of the transition from a standing position to a floor position and back again, you need feel no necessity to include this sequence in your yoga practice. If you have been able to do the twenty-five exercises in this book, you have performed most of the movements individually already, and it would be foolish to undo the sense of peace and relaxation that yoga can bring by straining

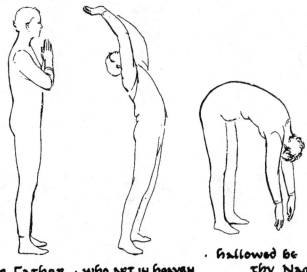

Our Father · who art in heaven · hallowed be thy Name.

Thy kingdom come.

thy will be done · on earth as it is in heaven.

Give us this day
our daily bread.

·And forgive us our trespasses,
as we forgive those
who trespass against us.

And lead us
not into temptation,
but deliver us from evil.

For thine is the Kingdom,
and the power.   · and the glory · for ever and ever.
                                                    Amen.

to accomplish something that is beyond you. And you can certainly pray the Lord's Prayer without performing the Salute to the Sun!

Our Father, who art in heaven

Stand in good alignment, with hands clasped in a position of prayer. Inhale as your arms reach straight forward with the palms down, and up above you in a big arc, and let the top of the spine bend slightly backward (see Easy Back Bend). Think of God, the Creator of earth and sky and all that is; you are God's creation, God's child.

Hallowed be Thy Name

Now exhale and reverse the arc, bringing the arms up, forward, and down, as the body stretches forward and then relaxes downward toward the earth, with the head and arms hanging loose (see Standing Forward Bend). You are paying homage to the One you worship.

Thy kingdom come

Bend the knees, place the palms of the hands on either side of the feet, inhale, and reach back with the right leg, like a sprinter about to begin a race. This active position is like a preparation for the future: God's kingdom.

Thy will be done

Exhale and bring the left leg back alongside the right leg and push back a little bit with your hands, so that your body is in a reverse "V" and the weight is divided between the legs and arms. (For an added stretch, push the weight backward toward your feet.) You are like a bridge in this position: often *we* are the bridge between the will of God and its accomplishment on earth.

(This position is sometimes done with the body straight, but I prefer the symmetry which the "bridge" contributes to the sequence.)

On earth as it is in heaven

Bring the knees down to the earth and slide into the next position as you inhale, by curving the spine and trying to bring the chest as close as possible to the ground as you straighten the body out along the ground (see The Cat #2). Really notice the contact of the knees with the earth, as you pray the word "earth."

Give us this day our daily bread
Keeping the hands on either side of the shoulders, palms down on the floor, inhale and raise the head and the upper body, looking toward the sky (see The Cobra). This is a position of humility, in which we remember the source of our life and, ultimately, of life's necessities.

And forgive us our trespasses as we forgive those who trespass against us
Exhale and push with the arms until you are again on hands and knees. Continue to push yourself up into the "bridge" position. (You may have to bring your hands back a few inches along the floor as you do this.) This is a position of penitence, and of making a connection or "bridge" between God's forgiveness and our forgiveness of others.

And lead us not into temptation but deliver us from evil
Inhale and bring the right foot forward until you are again in the "sprinter's position." (The next time you do the Salute, you can use the left leg both here and in "Thy kingdom come.") Look upward, as you think of God, your sustainer and deliverer.

For Thine is the kingdom and the power
Exhale and bring the left foot forward to meet the right foot. Inhale and begin to return to an upright position, bringing the arms straight forward and up above your head as you do so. Feel the sweep of the movement, as you meditate upon the glory of God.

And the glory, forever and ever
With the arms straight over the head, bend the top of the spine backward slightly, as you look toward the sky.

Amen

Exhale and straighten the body. Bring your arms forward until about chest level, then place them palms together in prayer position.

Check the body's alignment. Your body weight is centered over the earth. You, "bodyspirit," are centered in God.

VI

Relaxation

I lie down in peace. . . . for you alone, my God, make me dwell in safety.
(PSALM 4:8)

An integral part of Christian yoga practice is the period of progressive relaxation that follows the exercises. To prepare for the relaxation, you may wish to put on some extra clothing, such as a sweater, or to cover yourself with a blanket, because your body's metabolism will be slowing down. Lie on a mat or on a thick carpet, with the legs either straight out along the floor or, if that is a strain on the back, bent at the knees. (For some people, this position is easier on the back.) The arms should be relaxed on the floor, about three to four inches from your sides.

Feel the floor supporting the body; feel the heaviness of the body. Notice the breath. Imagine that you can see the breath as it enters and leaves the nostrils. Breathe normally, but consciously focus the breathing in the abdominal region.

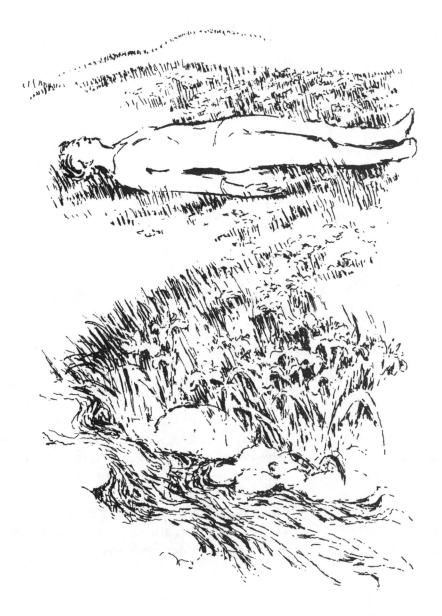

Now, beginning with the toes, consciously relax each part of the body in turn. If it helps you to do so, you can tense each part in turn and then relax it, or move each part in turn and then relax it. Some people, on the other hand, find that it is most relaxing just to send a silent message to the part of the body you wish to relax.

Relax: the right foot, the right calf, the right thigh; the left foot, the left calf, the left thigh. Relax the buttocks, the abdomen, the rib cage, and the chest. Relax the muscles of the back, and let all of the tension drain from the spine. Relax the right shoulder, the right upper arm, the right forearm, and the right hand. Relax the left shoulder, the left upper arm, the left forearm, and the left hand. Relax the front of the neck, and the back of the neck. Relax the jaw. Relax the cheeks. Relax the area around the eyes, the area between the eyebrows, the forehead, and the scalp.

Check over the body again for tension, and release any that you discover. Think of the inner organs of the body relaxing and the mind relaxing.

Notice your breath; "watch" it as it enters and leaves the nostrils.

Relaxation is itself a form of prayer. It expresses *trust;* it acknowledges that we are dependent upon a dependable God. Through physical relaxing, we can learn spiritual and psychological relaxation, releasing our need to be always in control. As we free our muscles from tension, we can free our spirits from anxiety. This relaxation exercise expresses kinetically our willingness to be part of *God's* plan, *God's* energy, and *God's* joy.

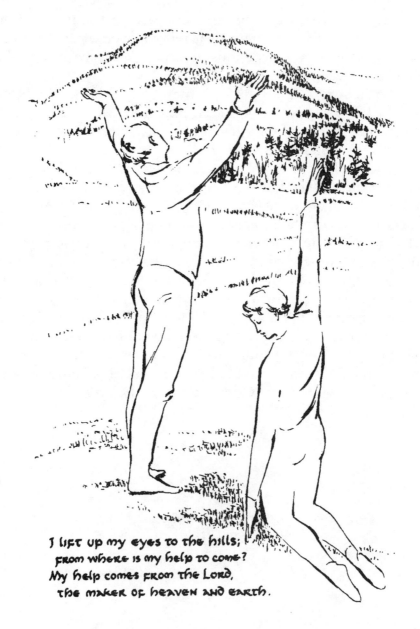

I lift up my eyes to the hills;
  from where is my help to come?
My help comes from the Lord,
  the maker of heaven and earth.

VII

Meditation

I wait for you, O God, my soul waits for you,
in your word is my hope.
(PSALM 130:4)

Meditation is a means of relaxing and focusing the mind, much as the physical exercises of yoga are a means of relaxing and focusing the body. Traditionally it is a standard part of yoga practice. For a person practicing meditation within a religious tradition, the purpose of that focusing is to center the whole attention on God. Thus, meditation is a form of prayer. This kind of prayer has been called contemplative prayer and centering prayer as well as meditation. It involves a paradox: the paradox that attention to the inmost self is also attention to God. The Trappist monk and writer Thomas Merton writes, "The fact is...that if you descend into the depths of your own spirit...and arrive somewhere near the center of what you *are,* you are confronted with the inescapable truth that, at the very root of your existence, you are in constant and immediate and inescapable contact with the infinite power of God."

The practices of yoga, relaxation, and meditation help us join together body and spirit in our search for God, who is a God of paradoxes. God is intimately within us and yet infinitely beyond us. God is revealed and yet unknown, the creator God of power and the self-emptying God who became flesh, the God whom we celebrate in the beauty of the worship of Christian community and the God whose face we see in the faces of the poor and the dispossessed of the world.

As we become acquainted with the mystery of our own "bodyspirit," we can grow in knowledge and in love of our God of paradox and of mystery. Focusing the mind and the heart in the practice of meditation is a means of exploration both of our own nature and of the mystery of God.

It is important to realize that in undertaking this exploration we need have no fear. Meditation has been called a "coming home" to what is most real and most basic about our human natures. We may discover things we had never noticed before—but they are probably parts of us we need to uncover. And since the journey's goal is to build our relationship with the God both within and beyond us, we are making that journey in good company—in God's company.

This chapter cannot be a treatise on the art of meditation—that can be found in many other books, including my *Breath of God*. But some simple guidelines are offered here that will help integrate this form of prayer into your physical practice.

First, if you are doing yoga on your own, be sure to save time for meditation at the conclusion of your practice. If you are part of a yoga class and wish to have more time for meditation and prayer than the class provides, you may wish to go into a church or some other quiet place for a period after the class is over.

To begin meditation, after you have relaxed completely, focus first on your breathing, as if you were watching the air enter and leave the nostrils. This focus alone is a very widely taught method of meditation, for the breath is not only a "kinetic" or movement-oriented focus, but the symbol and sign of God's spirit and life within you. You will notice your breath slowing down and becoming shallower during the meditation period, reflecting the peaceful state of both body and spirit.

You may wish, in addition, to repeat silently a word or phrase of your own choosing along with each breath. Such a word or phrase is called a *mantra*. Favorite mantras include "Jesus Christ," "My Lord and my God," "Holy Spirit," "Be still and know that I am God," or merely the word "God." You may have your own favorite phrase from scripture. The anonymous author of the fourteenth-century treatise *The Cloud of Unknowing* compares such a mantra to an "arrow" that we shoot through a "cloud of unknowing" toward God. The arrow's momentum is our desire for God.

Some people prefer "imaging": picturing an object such as a candle flame or cross, or a scene such as a beautiful outdoors scene or a chapel. Others find it more helpful to *look* at an actual object, such as a crucifix, a beautiful flower arrangement, or a picture, such as the drawing that follows this chapter. The use of *icons* in the Orthodox tradition is an example of this kind of gazing as a means to meditation.

Holding or touching an object, such as a smooth stone or rosary, is helpful to many. The fragrance of incense or pine needles takes some people to a place of inner stillness.

The possibilities are limitless, and you may wish to try various points of focus for a period of time until you find the one that best suits you. These points of focus are not the *end* but the *means* of "aiming" our desire toward God, like the "arrows" of *The Cloud of Unknowing*. They are also a means of gently returning our attention to the matter at hand—prayer—when our minds begin to wander, as they inevitably will!

It should be mentioned that the discipline of yoga is also an excellent preparation for other ways of prayer, such as intercessory prayer and reflection upon scripture. But this material I have covered in another book.

A further way of prayer you can incorporate into your yoga practice is what could be called Christian body prayer. We have suggested throughout this book that the yoga exercises themselves can become a form of prayer, as you move your body to the glory of the God who created you. The relaxation period can be a prayer of trust and gratitude, expressing "into your hands I commend my spirit"—and body!

In addition, you can be creative in expressing your prayer with your body. You have seen how the *body* can influence the *spirit*. Now explore how the *spirit* can influence the *body*. In other words, how can you express through physical action or posture the petitions and thanksgivings, sighs and laughter, of the spirit?

In Exercise 1, you have been introduced to a "movement mantra": that of "Father, Son, and Holy Spirit," or "Creator, Redeemer, and Sanctifier." Find another phrase or word, repeat it inwardly, in the rhythm of your breath, and discover what movement comes from *within* you to express that mantra. Then repeat the movement, over and over, until the prayer virtually becomes part of you.

You have already seen that a verbal prayer, such as the Lord's Prayer, can be expressed in movement. Find another prayer that means a great deal to you and explore what movements best express the parts of that prayer. They need not be strenuous—you may wish to move with the arms or hands alone.

You may wish to "move" through a story from scripture. Read the passage imaginatively, putting yourself in the place of each person in the story. Then move as each person would have moved. My first experience with such an exercise was in a movement workshop where we enacted the story of the raising of Lazarus. In turn, we experienced the roles of Martha, Mary, Jesus, the onlookers, and Lazarus through our bodily movement. In our final "movement meditation," I was Lazarus, and I will never forget the life coursing through my body upon being "summoned forth" by "Jesus," who happened to be a burly six-foot-tall Jesuit. The story, needless to say, was forever transformed for me, because I had experienced through *my* "bodyspirit," a story which I had hitherto experienced only through my imagination and intellect.

A fertile source of Christian body prayer is the Psalter. Take a psalm and express each verse in turn. The psalms encompass the whole range of human emotion, and, since they are poetry, they include many images. The drawing at the beginning of this chapter illustrates a movement meditation on Psalm 121: "I lift up my eyes to the hills. From whence does my help come? My help comes from the Lord, who made heaven and earth."

A further way of "praying with the body" is closer to nonverbal, contemplative prayer. It is merely a matter of taking the posture that most conveys the way you are feeling right now before God: *whatever* it is—from humble and quiet to open and exultant, from intense and beseeching to relaxed and accepting.

Take time, and enjoy the time, as you find your own ways of praying with the body, of integrating "bodyspirit" in your speaking to God, listening to God, and waiting upon God.

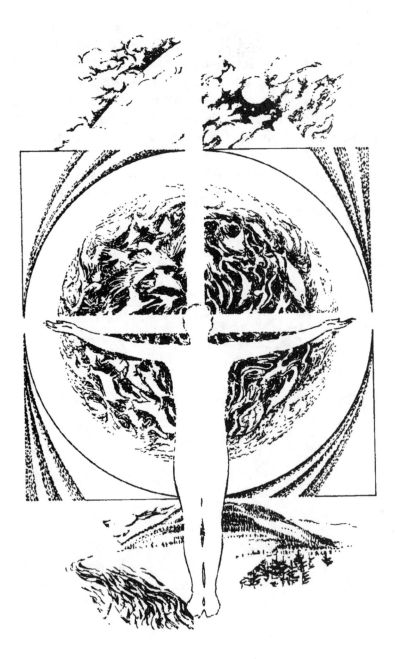

VIII

Christian Yoga Through the Day

Yours is the day, yours also the night.
(PSALM 74:15)

As you gain a sense of your own unity of "bodyspirit," it is likely that your perception of the world around you will change. If you really understand that your physical self is a holy thing, it is difficult to disregard the physical selves of others, whether they be the urban poor you pass on the sidewalk on a daily basis or the impoverished or persecuted people of other lands with whom you come in contact through the news media.

If you really understand the sacredness of God's creation, it will be difficult to disregard the wastefulness with which most of us live. One of the "yogas," or yokes, that I hope this book will help to encourage is a transformation of consciousness about our responsibilities regarding the earth. We are profoundly connected to our planet and to one another.

As we explore our "inner environment" through the attentiveness of Christian yoga, we need always to make the connection to the outer environment, both the people with whom we share the planet and the planet itself, our island home. As we learn to breathe properly, we need to find ways to preserve the very atmosphere upon which we depend. As we learn to relax our physical and spiritual tensions, we need to work and pray for relaxation of the tensions of poverty, injustice, and violence that divide the world's peoples.

The transformation must begin with each one of us, and on a simple day-to-day basis. There are many ways of integrating what you have learned in these pages into your daily life: creating a "yoga" or yoke that connects your prayer and your bodily life. To illustrate what I mean, we will imagine that you are in a profession that requires commuting to an office, and point out typical moments of your day.

Immediately upon awaking, turn your attention to your breath; let the breath become a prayer of thankfulness for a new day and for the air you breathe. Notice what parts of your body want to stretch—and stretch them. Get out of bed by rolling onto your side before putting your feet down over the side of the bed. If you are a "morning person," this time before breakfast may be the best time for your yoga practice and meditation. In any case, you may wish to choose a few exercises with which to begin the day, followed by a least a few moments of silence in which to offer the day to God.

Take advantage of commuting time between home and work. When you are walking, notice the weight of the body shifting from foot to foot. If you are sitting on a train, bus, or subway, use the opportunity to "center" by focusing on your breathing and making this time a period for meditation. If you find yourself standing while waiting for or riding public transportation, adjust your alignment. Notice your spine stretched toward the sky and the gentle inhalation and exhalation of your breathing. If you are driving, practice abdominal breathing, especially at traffic lights and in traffic jams, which can be a cause of stress and of the consequent shallow, rapid breathing.

In traveling to work, try to keep a sense of perspective about time. Ideally, allow yourself enough time so that the journey is not hurried or harried, despite the rush of those around you.

Often the early morning hours expose us to distressing sights—on the television news, in the newspaper, or on the streets. Hold those in need before God, knowing that you are profoundly connected to them.

Before you begin your work, look over your appointment book, holding each activity in turn before God. At the moment of beginning work, and at the beginning of each new task, take a few deep breaths to help you center your attention on the task at hand.

During the day, remain aware of your body as a "temple of the Spirit" and respect its needs. If you work long hours at a desk or computer, your muscles will probably send you messages of strain or fatigue. Pay attention to those messages; get up and move around or stretch periodically. Exercise 2, adapted for a seated position, and the head and shoulder rolls and rear arm lifts help release neck and shoulder tension. Rotating the feet at the ankles and free-form stretching of arms and legs help to alleviate the stiffness and fatigue that come from long periods of sitting. Both the Runner's Lunge (see "Thy Kingdom Come" on page 76) and the Modified Runner's Lunge (see page 74) will help release tension around the hip joints.

Respect, as well, the needs of others with whom you work. Remember that they, too, are unique creatures of God, every single person different from you—which, of course, provides interest but also the potential for conflict. If a stressful situation arises, remember the gift you have from God—your breath. Noticing your breath, exhaling your tension, and attempting to keep the breath regular and tranquil will help to calm you physiologically and also remind you to keep the situation in perspective.

Throughout the day, try to remember the sense of "timeless-ness" which you have learned in yoga practice. This does not mean that you will never get anything done! Rather, you will gain efficiency by attending to your tasks *one at a time,* laying aside worry about the work you have just finished and anxiety about the duties ahead. There *will* be enough time to finish everything that is really important. Discover your priorities in the light of your faith. You may well find that much of what you thought was important no longer seems so, but is merely a reaction to cultural expectations that have little to do with living fully and responsibly. For example, working overtime merely in order to make enough money to keep up with the Joneses makes little sense if it deprives us of our most precious commodity: time to spend on the things most important to us.

At the end of work, offer the day's accomplishments—and frustrations—to God, and leave them. Let the trip home be a real transition from your work-time. On public transportation, you can nap, read, or meditate. If you are driving, use the time for special music, tapes, or CDs to which you can look forward, or for calming silence.

If you are exhausted after a long day's work, try some gentle yoga exercise, relaxation, and meditation—or even some vigorous aerobic exercise—as soon as you get home. You will be surprised how rejuvenating exercise can be. Then you will be able to enjoy your food and your evening's relaxation. You will have shed the tension of the day and can enter the quiet pleasure of the evening hours. Christian yoga could well serve as a useful alternative service of vespers for sedentary Christians.

If you have children, it is not quite as simple! Depending on their age, you can invite them to join you in exercise, relaxation, and meditation, or explain that you need ten to fifteen minutes for your own private time—even a short period can be rejuvenating. Or join them in something *they* love, such as a game of basketball or a walk around the block, and do so in such a spirit that it becomes your vespers!

If you have difficulty sleeping, go through the progressive relaxation, as you visualize yourself relaxing "in God." Let God take care of your personal anxieties and your concerns for the world during the night. They will be in more able hands than yours.

Variations on these ideas apply to all lifestyles. A young parent at home with children, faced with innumerable tasks and interruptions, has many opportunities to focus on the present moment and to attend to one thing at a time, even if that one thing is likely to be interrupted by a telephone call or a toddler. Observe your children; you will learn much from them about using the body and about keeping a relaxed spirit. I have had children in my classes respond so immediately to the needs of their bodies that, when they feel tired, they lie down in the middle of a floor full of dancing children!

Let your tasks become a "yoga." Each moment and each task can be a "sacrament"—an "outward and visible sign of an inward and spiritual grace"—if we allow it to reveal God by giving it our prayerful attention. For example, lay aside any sense of time pressure and do the dishes in order to do the dishes, not to get the task over. You may be surprised that you will find new joy in simple physical tasks.

Look for connections between your actions and your prayer as you go about your daily activities. When I was in high school, I remember our parish priest advising us to say a prayer of thanksgiving every time we went up the school staircase and of penitence every time we went down—advice that obviously made quite an impression upon me, as it was offered some years ago! Look for your own connections. A prayer of cleansing and healing as you shower. Prayers of intercession for each member of your family as you fold their newly laundered clothes. Prayers of protection for the environment as you work in the garden or walk to work. Prayers of thanksgiving for the gifts the earth provides as you prepare food.

Then connect your prayer to your life in further ways, through simple actions. Express your love for the earth by planting a small organic vegetable garden or growing some herbs in flowerpots on a window sill. Express your solidarity with the poor by volunteering to work in a soup kitchen one day a week, or by refusing to buy food items that are produced under dehumanizing conditions. Express a sense of human community by writing a "thank you" when one is not necessarily expected, or by telephoning a lonely acquaintance. Express joy in God's creation by going for a walk and really noticing the things around you. These suggestions do not begin to exhaust the ways you can live your life "from the inside," just as you practice your yoga movements "from the inside." The prayer that inspires action and the action that inspires prayer will themselves become a "yoga," as they intertwine in an ongoing rhythm of unity in your life, expressing what you know of God's life within you and within the world.

Christian yoga unites us to the joy whose source is the knowledge of God's life within us. Praise God for the gift of that life in your body, your "bodyspirit." This body has been given us for a time; we need to care for it and use it responsibly, so that with it we can continue God's creative, healing work in a world in sore need. My hope is that this book has enabled you in some way to do so, as well as to grow in knowledge and love of God.